This edition first published by Ravette Books Limited 1988.

Printed and bound for Ravette Books Limited,
3 Glenside Estate, Star Road,
Partridge Green, Horsham,
Sussex RH13 8RA
by Purnell Book Production Limited
Paulton, Bristol
A member of BPCC plc

ISBN: 1 85304 061 4

"A BORN LEADER"

"AN EXPERT IN BUSH CRAFT"

PEANUTS featuring "Good ol' Charlie Brown" by Schulz

4-20

PEANUTS

featuring

"Good ol' CharlieBrown"

by SCHULZ

"AROUND THE OLD CAMPFIRE"

"AT HOME IN THE GREAT OUTDOORS"

5-4

POP!

KLUNK!

I HAVE A STRANGE TEAM..

PEANUTS

featuring "Good ol' Charlie Brown"

by SCHULZ

type
TYPE
type
type
TYPE

I'LL BET YOU FORGOT, DIDN'T YOU?

TODAY IS MOTHER'S DAY!

"A GOOD BEAGLE SCOUT SHOWS THE WAY"

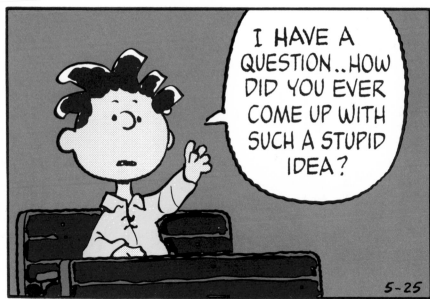

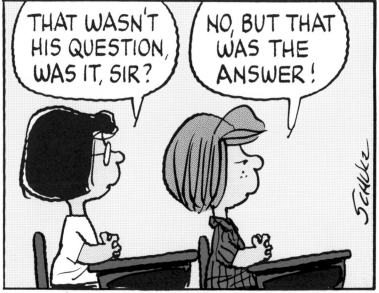

"A (NOT SO) CLEVER DISGUISE"

"THE ONE THAT DIDN'T GET AWAY"

PEANUTS

featuring "Good ol' Charlie Brown"

by SCHULZ

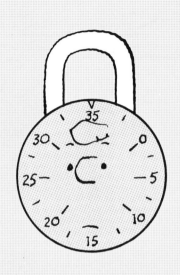

WHAT'S THIS?

THESE ARE OUR NEW SAFETY DESKS, CHARLIE BROWN

SAFETY DESKS?

OKAY, PARTNER, NOW!

6-8

I DON'T HAVE ANY SHOELACES.. I DON'T EVEN HAVE ANY SHOES!

NOW, PARTNER! I SAID, "NOW!"

© 1986 United Feature Syndicate, Inc.

IT HURTS WHEN YOU TIE YOUR TOES TOGETHER!

"LIVING IN THE FLIGHT PATH"

"THAT'S WHAT LIFEGUARDS ARE FOR."

"A LYRICAL DISCUSSION"

" HORSE-PLAY "

PEANUTS featuring "Good ol' Charlie Brown"

by SCHULZ

"DEAR DAD..WELL, HERE WE ARE AT CAMP REMOTE.."

I THINK THEY PRONOUNCE IT "REMOTAY," SIR

I SWEAR, SIR, THAT I CAN HARDLY STAND IT!

I MAY JUST PUSH HIM IN THE LAKE OR SOMETHING!

AFTER ALL, I CAME TO CAMP TO HAVE A GOOD TIME, DIDN'T I?

7-6

"A TAKE HOME DOGGIE BAG"

THERE'S A BOYS' CAMP ACROSS THE LAKE, SIR..DO YOU THINK CHARLES IS THERE?

CHARLES! ARE YOU OVER THERE?

MARCIE! THAT'S EMBARRASSING!

7-13

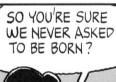

"LOOK - NO WINGS!"

PEANUTS
featuring
"Good ol' Charlie Brown"
by Schulz

Class of 1986

HOW DO I LOOK?

VERY NICE

WHERE ARE YOU GOING?

OUR KINDERGARTEN CLASS IS HAVING A REUNION..

IT SHOULD BE INTERESTING TO SEE HOW MUCH EVERYONE HAS CHANGED..

© 1986 United Feature Syndicate, Inc. 12-7

WELL, HOW WAS THE REUNION?

FINE! I HAD A GOOD TIME.. IT WAS NICE SEEING EVERYONE AGAIN

BUT YOU KNOW WHAT SURPRISED ME? NONE OF THE GUYS WERE BALD!

"WOODSTOCK AT THE HELM"

PEANUTS featuring "Good ol' CharlieBrown" by Schulz

I HEAR FOOTSTEPS

HEY, SNOOPY, LET'S GO FOR A WALK!

© 1986 United Feature Syndicate, Inc.

THIS IS THE WAY IT WAS MEANT TO BE

A BOY AND HIS DOG HIKING LIKE PERFECT COMRADES THROUGH THE WOODS

IF YOU SEE A SQUIRREL, OR A DEER, OR A PHEASANT OR A RABBIT, PLEASE FEEL FREE TO BARK AND HOWL AND PURSUE THEM MADLY OVER THE HILLS, THROUGH THE STREAMS AND ACROSS THE FIELDS!

12-14

I HATE IT WHEN HE LOOKS AT ME LIKE THAT..

"HEAVEN ON A STICK"

PEANUTS by SCHULZ

IT'S A LETTER FROM YOUR BROTHER SPIKE

GOOD OL' SPIKE!

Dear Snoopy,

Just thought I'd drop you a line to let you know how I've been doing.

My Western Art hasn't been selling as well as I had hoped

SALE SALE

Sometimes I think maybe I'm not a good businessman.

1-18

Therefore, I'm trying to concentrate on organization and leadership.

© 1987 United Feature Syndicate, Inc.

I SUPPOSE YOU'RE ALL WONDERING WHY I'VE ASKED YOU HERE TODAY...

SCHULZ

"ENCOUNTERING A FRIENDLY NATIVE"

"THE BEAGLE SCOUT CHECKS HIS MAP"

" PRACTICE MAKES PERFECT "

PEANUTS
by Schulz

SPIKE'S BEEN WRITING TO YOU A LOT LATELY, HASN'T HE?

SPIKE LEADS A VERY ACTIVE LIFE

Dear Brother Snoopy, I think everyone should know more of the desert and our way of life.

Two days ago I made a time capsule.

What could I put in it that would be of interest to a future age?

My hat, of course!

2-15

Five thousand years from now another civilization will be able to see what we wore on the desert.

TIME CAPSULE DO NOT OPEN UNTIL 6987!

That night it got very cold.

The next day I opened the time capsule.
Love, Spike

© 1987 United Feature Syndicate, Inc.

PEANUTS.
by Schulz

THIS IS MY REPORT ON GEORGE WASHINGTON, WHO WAS BORN IN 1732..

AS A SPECIAL TREAT FOR ALL OF YOU, I HAVE DRAWN HIS PORTRAIT...

WHAT?

IT LOOKS LIKE WHO?

2-22

WHEN WAS HE BORN?

REALLY?

OKAY, MOVING ON TO 1809...

SCHULZ

"WE ALL NEED A SENSE OF DIRECTION"

HERE'S THE WORLD WAR I FLYING ACE WALKING ALONG A COUNTRY ROAD IN FRANCE...

3-1

AH! A BEAUTIFUL FRENCH LASS APPROACHES..

QUICKLY HE CONSULTS HIS PHRASE BOOK..

BONJOUR, MONSIEUR!

I'LL ASK HER IF SHE'D LIKE TO GO GET SOME FRENCH TOAST..

Y A-T-IL LONGTEMPS QUE VOUS ÊTES EN FRANCE?

MAYBE SHE'D LIKE TO GO GET SOME FRENCH FRIES..HOW DO YOU SAY THAT?

COMMENT TROUVEZ-VOUS PARIS?

BOISSAY

JE TROUVE PARIS TRÈS BEAU!

WHAT'S SHE SAYING?

DE QUEL RÉGIMENT ÊTES-VOUS?

I CAN'T FIND FRENCH TOAST..

© 1987 United Feature Syndicate, Inc.

SOYEZ SAGE.. PORTEZ-VOUS BIEN

WAIT! HOW ABOUT A TACO?

"A WEEKENDER TO REMEMBER"

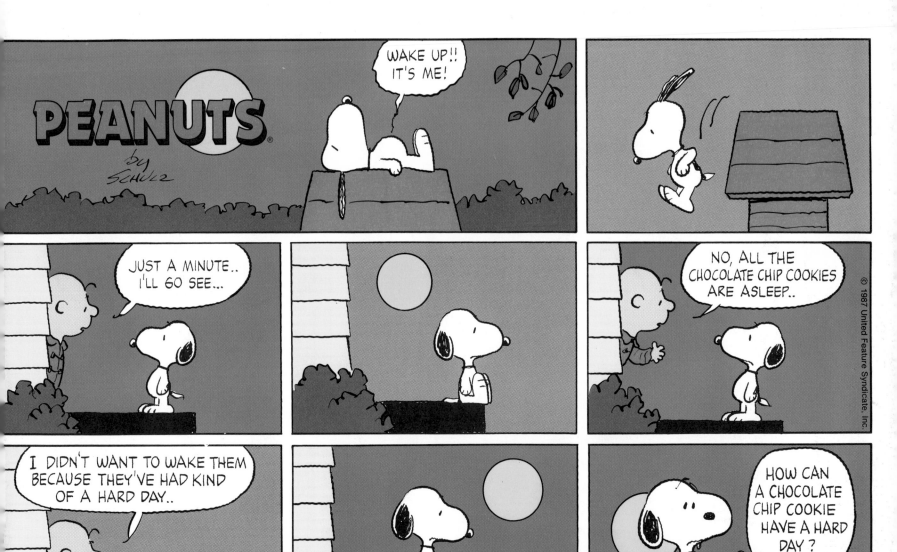

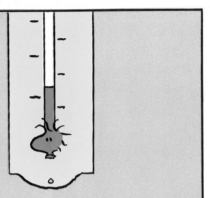